PRAISE THE KING OF GLORY

Other titles by Duane L. Herrmann

Whispers Shouting Glory
Voices from a Borrowed Garden, ed.
Fasting, The Moon and its Suns, ed.
Early Bahá'ís of Enterprise
The Bahá'í Faith in Kansas since 1897
The Life of May Brown
The Bahá'í Community of Samarkand
By Thy Strengthening Grace
Hidden Meanings in the Poetry
       of Robert Hayden
Blessings of Teaching
Prairies of Possibilities
Ichnographical: 173
Institor Gleg: short stories

Praise the King of Glory

New and Selected Poems

Duane L. Herrmann

©2017 / 173, 2020 / 177 Duane L. Herrmann

ISBN: 978-1-879448-00-1
          1-879448-00-9

Corrected: 2020

Cover assembled by Trosten B. Herrmann.

Buffalo Press

Topeka, KS

CONTENTS

Foreword

The poems you will find here express the yearnings of a heart and mind on a spiritual quest for closeness with the "King of Glory" and the "Traceless Friend," references to the Manifestation of God for this age, as well as God. Depicting both the wonders and the vicissitudes of the spiritual journey and calling, they remind us of the importance of this quest— the joy and radiance of it, the hope of fulfillment, the questions, the choices, the sacrifices, the agony of separation. Woven through the poet's words are quotations from the Bahá'í Revelation, showing how close he is on the path of daily seeking, of hoping to attain "the Distant Shore." Metaphorically, the scent of rose petals wafts from these pages, and one admires the certitude of the poet's convictions. The final affirmation, "I die content," is a hope we all share, and the poems may well help us to achieve that goal as we contemplate their meaning and strive to live more fully in awareness of spirit.

Many of these poems, for instance about the stone in the hand of the woman, bring events to life in an effective way. I cried as I read some of these poems. It is important to connect personally with the lives of the Messengers of God and feel them deeply. We need more such poems!

Anne Perry, Ph.D.
2020

Introduction:

This volume of new and selected poems has been published to celebrate the bicentennial of the birth of Bahá'u'lláh, Prophet-Founder of the Bahá'í Faith. Many of the poems refer to events in the life of Bahá'u'lláh. For this reason, a brief sketch of His life can be found in the back of this volume.

The Guardian of the Bahá'í Faith encouraged Bahá'ís to include poetry in their meetings. He specifically mentioned poems based on the Holy Words, or inspired by them. Such poems can elevate the hearts. Many of the poems here have some connection to Bahá'í Sacred Texts, even quoting from them. It is hoped that this collection may contribute toward that aspiration.

POEMS

TO THE ENDS...

Searching high and low –
   in field and forest,
over plains and seas,
   over marsh and mountain,
where is that
   which will fill my soul?
"...if thou searchest the universe
   forever more,
thy quest
   will be in vain."

What...
   will make me whole?
"...thou mayest find Me
   standing within thee,
mighty, powerful
   and self-subsisting."

Within my heart
   all this time!

HASTEN, THOU

"Hasten...
that thou mayest
become
an
immortal soul."

Hasten –
do not tarry
on the earthly
plane,
your destiny
is nobler.

Hasten,
flee this life,
your role is brief
yet
significant
and loved.

BAHÁ'U'LLÁH

Oh, Bahá'u'lláh,
Oh, Bahá'u'lláh,
  my heart sings...

Oh, Bahá'u'lláh,
Oh, Bahá'u'lláh
  my soul rejoices...

When I behold Thy Love –
When I contemplate Thy Beauty –
When I realize Thy Mercy –

Thy Light shines,
illumines life
and makes me whole.

Oh, Bahá'u'lláh,
Oh, Bahá'u'lláh,
  I can say no more...

Oh, Bahá'u'lláh...

Thy Glory...

Bahá...

WITH ME

The Revelation of Bahá'u'lláh is with me

In front of me,
    and behind me.
To my right,
    and to my left.
Above me,
    and below me –
All around:

In my soul,
Pulsing in my veins,
In the very air I breathe,

Giving light and vision to my eyes,
Giving music and sweetness to my ears,
Giving praise and thanksgiving to my lips,

Giving courage, strength and joy to my heart,
Giving inspiration, power and clarity to my mind,
Giving existence, exaltation and eternity to my soul.

Praised be, the Greatest Name!!

THE YEAR HIN

In darkness, rustling
   moaning silence,
captives locked in chains
   sit in filth.

Holy Chanting rings
   echoes up and out:
"God is sufficient unto me,
   He verily is the All-sufficing."
and response:
   "In Him let the trusting trust."

Terror to the king
   who hears and reigns.

Amidst the darkness stench
   Angel's vision shines:
Awake!!
   Man like no other.
Precious Being, now:
   the ages have arrived.

And all the atoms cry aloud:
   the universe renewed,
realities concealed are manifest.
   Gloryannas ring.

>

The world passed away
   in slumber and in death.
Patience, patience,
   for the Year Hin –

the World will begin.

Note p.114

MAID OF HEAVEN

Maiden in the air
   suspended,
a Being between this world
   and Reality,
pointing, she proclaimed
   the Voice of God:
"We shall render Thee victorious
   by Thy self and by Thy pen."
Her Light was seen
   by none but one
in chains and filth –
   the captive King of Glory.

True words as time
   reveal their splendor,
souls respond, embrace, arise
   to aid His Pen
and reconstruct
   hearts and lives and planets.

BEST BELOVED OF THE WORLDS

Victorious by Thyself
    and by Thy pen,
Treasures of the earth
    God will raise up
to aid Thee,
    through Thy Name,
to revive the hearts
    of all mankind.

A mighty torrent,
    flowed from crown to breast,
from the lofty mount
    to set Thy limbs on fire.

Asleep upon Thy couch,
    a man like others,
breezes flowed and taught
    knowledge of all things.

A leaf on the winds
    of the Will of God.

THE STONE'S ACCOUNT

I am a simple stone:
  rough and dull,
no color to note,
  but fit for a hand.
I had an honor,
  once,
to touch a holy
  precious being.
He was walking,
  under guard,
and a woman cried
  for them to stop.
Love personified,
  he stood for her.
I was in her hand
  and she threw me.
For just a moment
  I touched Glory!

THAT JOURNEY

That winter journey
in the pain of cold
wind tearing through
thin clothes
one can never forget –
and no one will.
That epic journey
resounds and will continue:
howdahs crude, primitive,
no match
for modern transportation.
Yet that journey
is the one remembered
when all others,
but that of Abraham,
are forgotten.

Forever stumbling
over ice;
freezing wind
continuous howling
through the ages,
and we try
and stumble our way
to perfection
in echo
of that journey
forever through time.

FINAL VOYAGE

The boat languished in the bay,
there was no wind,
no water to drink,
no food
all that long, hot day.
We reached the shore,
the city, fort,
prison,
and a crowd was there
to great us,
revile us,
and pelt us
with garbage.
Patiently
we forbore.
Eventually,
eternally,
Glory Reigns!

GUARD DUTY

Day after day
watching waves
hit the seawall of the fort,
the most boring post
in the world,
the most desolate of cities,
far, far from home
and life and hope and love.
Waves crash in
water recedes
and the sea is flat forever.
Yesterday arrived here
God of the Persians,
the population cried
and reviled them
with garbage and with screaming.
But strangely,
He shone with Glory.

A GLIMPSE IN TIME

Waves break upon the wall,
  roughly in storm,
  softly when calm,
relentlessly, never ceasing.

Sea-damp fills the air,
  thick evening fog,
  hot humid day,
forever and unending.

In dead of night pale moonlight
  drifts across the floor,
  where shadow bars
weave silent signs of hate.

The weight upon His shoulders,
  a prisoner unknown,
  rejected by the world…
the Promised King at last.

'There is a power in this Cause…
  far, far, away,
  from the ken of men and angels…
the mystery of the Kingdom of Abhá!'

SILENT FOOTSTEPS PASSING

White walls remain, blue trim,
    pilgrim places, still and hushed.

Life of day-to-day, purpose and activity;
    moved on with time.

Unknown, excluded by the world
    the Promised King was here.

The solitary cell a witness – stark
    haunting echo of rejection.

Now monuments and memories
    proclaim the glorious state,

With terraced gardens rising
    from sea to deep blue sky,

Pulling minds and hearts
    to the Center Holy Spot.

Transformation is the Way of God:
    people, places, planets.

One day humankind will learn…
    God passed by us again.

GOLDEN ALCHEMY

Crucibles of pain
    transmute
        the clay
    into purest gold.

The fire cries:
    "Change, change;
        Melt away imperfection,
        Vaporize the mist.
    Luster gleaming
        shall
        be thy reward."

Searing soul experience:
    "I'm dying...
        I'm dying....
            I'm...."

        Gone.

The pieces don't remain,
    They now BE
        something new:

>

Re-created ones
   now speak
      new words,
      new forms,
      new vision.

A new song
   fills new hearts
   with new worlds.

GENESIS II

Neutrons explode!
Electrons dance in ecstasy
    and dissolve!
Protons expire in bliss.

All of creation
    is re-created in an instant.
Omnipotence unleashed:
    Genesis again,
through the power of the word:
    "BE!"
and it is done.

THIS is Riḍván!!
    Paradise and Divine Springtime.

Mere mortals move
    if they perceive
        the blinding knowledge:
Omnipotent NOW
    invoking new beings
to sustain the Mighty Word
unleashed
    to ravage the universe,
    destroy and rebuild.

>

Oneness is the basis,
    unity and peace result.

Riḍván: Dawn
  of the maturity
  of the human race.

RIḌVÁN, THE GLORIOUS

Who can imagine
the day has come
when ages have fulfilled
their long-awaited promise.
Joy abounds!!
The Lord of All has come.
Joy to the world!
The promise of all time
has been fulfilled!
Who can hesitate
or doubt?
Evidences all around
proclaim: This is the day!
The Day of God,
the Most Glorious!
Oh! Glorious Riḍván!
You have come
and we REJOICE!!

DESERT GROWING

A flower grows –
  a rose
    in the desert thicket.
Harsh life surrounds
  the fragrant rose:
    blossom – alone.
Praise the Rose
  and glorify its name:
    The All-Glorious.
The bloom inspires
  flowers, more,
    to open and bloom:
flowers make gardens,
  gardens
    of beauty and glory.
Desert gardens bloom
  and honor –
    Rose of Most Great Beauty.

RIḌVÁN: THE DAWN

The world is sleeping,
   in darkness
   ignorance
   and death.

Ages Pass.

Slightly, clouds are parted –
   Dawn begins.

A ray of light
   flickers here
   and there and there.
A few souls wake;
   the world
   remains in slumber.

Dawn proceeds.

Many are called
   to Truth
   and Light
   and Justice
     but few are chosen.

>

The wind moves among the world
    selecting one here,
            one there,
            another far away.

The dead wonder why
    and grow afraid.
    They do not understand.
Hate increases,
    crashing on the few:
    their souls sustain...

The Tree grows,
Beauty spreads:

Yes, Lord.
    I am here.

I pray to remain
    steadfast.

In His service.

SHRILL VOICE

The shrill voice
of the holy pen
calls betwixt
earth and heaven.

Who will listen?

Clerics?
In their rites performing
say words they don't believe,
not deeply.
Kings?
On their proud and fragile
thrones and pomp.
Ordinary people?
With oppression all around,
yearning for freedom
and their full potential
as growing, powerful
spiritual beings.

THE LIGHT AND THE SOUL

I.
Amid the darkness clouds
   the soul stumbles, confused, awry
in the dim:
      no direction, aim or hope.

The Light perceived is faint,
   unknown, unfocused.

The soul is dazed, confused
   without meaning or suggestion,
What matters? What way?
      What difference does it make?

The Light remains steadfast.

Darkness, doubt and anger:
   There is no purpose!
There is no reason!
      All is waste!!

Undimmed, the Light maintains...
   its position.

II.
Numb, the seeker flees imagination:
   horrors no one else
can devise, or see
      descending in the depths.

Pure intent guides the seeking
   earnest soul.

Faltering toward purpose
   formulating hope
the doubter overcomes despondence
      and orients to aim.

Faithful is the Light –
   and serene.

The seeker climbs rugged inclination
   overcomes deceit
fixates on reunion,
      and stifles doubt.

In Peace
   it waits.

III.
Impatience builds as gloom recedes,
   faintly in the mist is seen
the shape of perseverance
      and expectation of relief.

The Steady One contains
   energy for giving.

The seeking soul receives
   with open heart
the impulse to renew the pain
      of giving and to strive.

The Light receives and offers back
   bounties beyond belief.

The soul exults in blessedness
   and raises drops of joy.
The goal of journey, nearing: seen
      is precious sight indeed.

The Light impels belief
   and grants comprehension.
The lovers race, embrace
      and forswear all others.

Journey is reunion.

THE MOST GREAT DAY

Sitting on the lawn
  with tents,
the water of the lake
  softly laps
the shore as prayers
  carry on the wind.
It is the First Day of Felicity
  and the air is warm.
Carpets on the ground
  evoke the home
of the Promised One
  Who announced this Day
to surpass
  all other days.
The universe rejoiced
  and creation rang
with praise
  for this New Day!

RIḌVÁN CREATION

On the First Day of Riḍván
  the world was recreated.
From that point
  the present age began:
telephone,
  automobile, aeroplane,
radio and TV too –
  all from Riḍván.
The Glorious of Days,
  The King of Festivals,
that Point in Time
  from which all things
were made new
  and the earth
has never been the same
  and will continue
until such time
  as has no end.

SOUL MONARCH

The King of Glory
  reigns
  through chaos, confusion
   and transformation.

Weak lives –
Shattered cultures –
Broken hearts –
  are all transmuted
  into new creations.
Inward real,
  to the heart
   changes penetrate;
Rearranging molecules
  and atoms of the soul.

There is no end
  to maelstrom matrix,
   outside our power –
   comprehension.

Fortunate are they
  who fling themselves
  into process:
"Gold! Here I come –
  through the fiery furnace."
Alchemy of souls
   complete.

SOARING BIRD

Soaring bird,
  calling mankind – higher and higher
    to unseen realms of love and delight.
Opening eyes
  of hearts and minds
    to greater visions of glory and truth.
Summoning
  the souls to lose the chains and fetters
    of self that bind each heart.
Soaring high –
  into spaces and spirit worlds
    beyond imagination or belief.

CALLING...

Listen!
  the celestial cry:
    the Nightingale – of Paradise.

Come.
  COME!!

THE WORD IS ONE

Giving His sermon on the mount
Muhammad took a breath
and uttered timeless words.

Jesus stood in command
at the head of His army
to fight the true, inner jihad.

Jerusalem rang its bells
as Krishna rode the stallion
on the first of Ramadan.

The Gate of Glory opened
while drums and symbols
praised the Lord of Hosts.

Minarets of Byzantium sang
as Buddha raised his pen
and wrote immortal hymns.

Zoroaster strode the water
to launch Salvations Ark
upon the Sea of Self.

DOOR OF GRACE

At the Door of Thy Grace
  I stand,
humbly beseeching Thy Mercy
  I wait,
in thrall before Thy Throne
  I serve,
as a witness to Thy Truth
  I speak,
a banner of Thy Might
  I raise,
mankind, unto Thy Glory
  I call,
it is now, and always
  will be,
Thy Mercy and Thy Grace
  from Thee
to Thy creatures
  in need.

SURRENDER

The crystal air behind the "real"
   is truth in fact.
The oneness of <u>all</u> things –
   flowing power overwhelms
A little mind at prayer
   losing hold of one "reality."
Seeing peace beyond the war
   and fellowship transcendent.
Prayer inarticulate,
   is replaced by muffled sobs.
Some say, "crazy," others nod
   in wisdom of their years.
To pray, to give – surrender human will
   to one Benevolent One:
There is no other purpose, life,
   or direction for existence.
Soul-sated prayer – exhaustion,
   and collapse in exaltation.

FIRE AND SNOW

I.
Angels weep in separation,
    distant
  from the Court of Glory.

The fire of their love
    would consume them
  but for their tears.

Chained in bodies
    in the world of names,
  afflictions abound.

They yearn for peace,
    reunion and release
  from self.

Patience, patience:
    pain is fleeting,
  patience.

The journey,
    long,
  will end in bliss and union.

Time will come
    when time
  will be no more.

Peace and joy
    will be the prize
  for faithfulness.

In Glory, upon Glory
    and Light,
  forevermore.

II.
Thy strengthening Grace,
    Oh my God,
  will help them.

Thy protection,
    Oh Lord,
  will assist them.

Thy victory,
    Oh Redeemer,
  will hearten them.

Thy sovereignty,
    Oh Glory,
  will sustain them.

>

Thy Mercy,
   Oh All-Merciful,
  will forgive them.

For they are in need
   of Thy mercy, strength
  and assistance.

III.
Steadfastness
  in longing
  and faith,

In Glory, upon Glory
   and, forevermore:
  LIGHT!

Eternally
  be
  with them.

IN WONDER

Surging from the sky
singing praises
to the One
Who originated
all being,
came they.

Multitudes of praise
pour forth,
range upon range
in ecstasy.

Colors
transcending the rainbow
in waves
vibrantly
dancing
on air.

This is the living,
This is the joy,
This is the purpose
beyond breath.

IN THE DARKNESS SHINES

What manner of light,
in the darkness shines
unearthly and unreal?

Transcendent
and awe-spiring,
it glances on our lives.

In the darkness surely,
when the soul is tried.
We see the light most real.

This LIGHT,
illumination,
shows the way to grow.

In the darkness shines
the Light Divine
into the depths of pain.

For if we see,
we will transcend
the limits –
of our selves.

"And they have made their dwelling,
in the shadow of the Essence."

SUN MAGNIFICENT

Bahá'u'lláh:
the Sun Magnificent,
has rearranged the soul
and body and heart
of generations.

Dynamic destinies await
those millions who
fling themselves into the sun –
becoming stars.

Hesitation kills
the soul in some degrees:
Run! Leap! Jump!
Into life with God!

Bahá'u'lláh fulfills
the ancient need
and mystic union
with absolute reality
and sacredness.

Exaltation rings
from one so unattached;
transcendent,
leaving self
and nothingness.

>

Bahá'u'lláh, the Sun
consumes, renews, transforms
the dust
into Magnificence!

INVOCATION MEDITATION

"O Moving Form of Dust"
  Bahá'u'lláh addresses
    the created of this world.

"In the image and likeness of God
  He created him;
    male and female, He created them."

From the dust and "a moist germ,"
  to dust do we return,
    our shadow selves and bodies.

For, around us, all we see
  are dust constructions,
    none of which is 'real.'

The 'Real' lies ahead
  in worlds unknown and glorious
    when we leave this dust behind,

Find our true selves,
  mighty, spiritual beings:
    Spiritual Lights!

STEADFASTNESS

Toward the building of a world
that no one knows
and cannot see,
not even you or me.

A world beyond our farthest dreams –
but dreams can clash
and so can we.

A world beyond description –
but still our goal and aim;
we falter on

One step at a time
and we stumble and spill
yet we try
against all odds

Toward the building of a world
that no one knows
and cannot see,
not even you, or me.

GARDEN OF THE ROSE

The Garden of the Rose
summons wretched flowers
from the desert
for transformation:
liberation, resurrection,
and the chance to be a rose.

The Garden of the Rose
is open to all people.
Some pass by unseeing.
Some wander in then out.
Some stop to destroy –
they cannot live with Beauty.

The Garden of the Rose
is dwelt within by lovers –
lovers who cannot stay away;
lovers whose breath is fragrant
whose hearts are shining stars
whose souls are soaring birds.

The Garden of the Rose
endures supreme
with ancient Beauty.
Renewed from age to age
to rescue all lost flowers
and welcome each one home,

In the Garden of the Rose.

LIGHTLY TREADING

To be respectful of The Mother
we must step lightly
when walking on her.

Our treading must not be
a cause of sorrow or disruption;
for others must pass too.

Behind us we must leave
a trail of Beauty –
in faces, places, planets:

A trail of Beauty to resound
in Glory dancing on the waves
of human tracing.

SUPPLICATION

O My God.

O My Lord.

O My Master!

I beg Thee to forgive me
 for seeking:
 any pleasure
 save Thy love,
 any comfort
 except Thy nearness,
 any delight
 besides Thy good pleasure,
 any existence
 other than communion with Thee.

QUIET AND PEACE

Be still.
Silent
as a solitary cloud
in the sky,
or moon
full of light.

Be still.
Silent,
let it rest:
your mind
and your body;
let it rest.

Be still.
Silent,
from the depths
of the well
of peace:
let silence flow.

Be still.
Silent,
as the stars
in their courses
circling round
the planet.

>

Be still.
Silent,
breathe
slowly, softly,
with meaning
and grace.

Be still.
Silent,
rest,
as rocks repose
in their might
and strength.

Be still.
Silent,
as the flower opens
softly to the sun,
and glorifies
its Lord.

Be still.
Silent,
open to the Spirit
whispering
softly
in your heart.

>

Be still.
Silent
to the rhythm
and the flow
of the soul
of Bahá.

YES, LORD! – I COME

Waiting,
  afraid to sleep
    for the One in the Night.

Praying,
  day and night
    not to be left behind.

Hoping,
  with all my soul
    to be of the Chosen.

Loving,
  with all my heart
    God and Jesus, my Friend.

Waiting...
  Praying...
    Hoping...
      Loving...

My short years were endless,
  nights were late with longing;
    no sign of fulfillment,
    no light among the chaos.

>

waiting...
  praying...
    hoping...
      loving...

I stumbled –
  into the Gate of Golden Light.

I Knew.
This was <u>IT</u>!!

YES, LORD!

  I come.

FOR THE GLORY OF THY NAME

For the Glory of Thy Name,
I will sacrifice –
   my earthly desires,
   my animal passions,
      every irregular inclination.

For the Glory of Thy Name,
I will sacrifice –
   my selfish emotions,
   my wayward thoughts,
      every unbecoming idea.

For the Glory of Thy Name,
I will sacrifice –
   my time and resources,
   my life and love,
      and all that I may gain.

Millions have already given much:
   money, honor, family, home, and lives.

What can I give?

SOARING BIRD

Soaring bird,
  calling mankind – higher and higher
    to unseen realms of love and delight.

Opening eyes
  of hearts and minds
    to greater visions of glory and truth.

Summoning
  the souls to lose the chains and fetters
    of self that bind each heart.

Soaring high -
  into spaces and spirit worlds
    beyond imagination or belief.

CALLING...

Listen!
  the celestial cry:
    the Nightingale – of Paradise.

Come.
  COME!!

HERE AM I

Traveler on the road of life
   stumbles and falls
his life in pieces
   no where to turn,
no help in sight,
   despair is all he knows.
A ray of light shines through
   from an unknown source.
He follows the light
   and finds:
Worlds of Glory, Light,
   Peace and Joy!

"Oh Lord!!
   Increase my astonishment in Thee!"
"I am here, My Lord.
   Here am I!"

He found the home
   he never knew was there.

PLEASE GOD!

Oh, Bahá'u'lláh,
the aching in my heart
    cries from the depths of my soul
    in longing
    for my will to be Thine.

The anguish of my spirit
    is tearing my soul
    and rending my heart to shreds.

Please God,
    help me to sustain
    the transformation
    into a new creation.

Praised be the Greatest Name –
    the Power
    the Glory
    the Oneness.

There is no other answer,
    no other way.

CREATED FOR

Thou hast been created
    out of dust
to become
    a being of Light:
Light, Illumination
    and Glory of the world.
But coming from dust
    you will desire dust.
The challenge:
    to rise into the Light.
Each soul confronts
    same eternal choice
This is the struggle,
    this is the choice:
remain attached to dust
    or resist
and rise into
    Being of Light.

TO STRIVE

To strive to be the way we may
  eventually sing,
    is our desire.
To strive to live as if each day
  was most precious
    is our need.
To strive to say the kindest thought
  to bless another,
    is our gift.
To strive to learn the most we can
  about the daily grace,
    is our duty.
To strive to be alive to every hope
  for a world of peace:
    is necessity.
For we are all together one creation
  learning to love
    our One Creator.

I ASK

Have mercy on my soul,
    Dear God, PLEASE!
I have tried,
    only You know
how long and how hard
    I have been trying.
Please, God forgive
    my stupidities and self
absorbed times
    when I could have done more.
I am sorry,
    I beg You, God,
All-Merciful, to forgive
    this weak soul of mine.
I will try and I will fail,
    but I pray
that I will learn
    and fail less and less.
Please God,
    I beg Thee
with Thine aid
    and assistance
I can improve
    and grow stronger,
more mature, detached
    and wise.

>

Make of me, O God,
   a hollow reed
that I may show
   Your Glory all around.
Please God,
   let it be so.
I ask in Thy Name,
   the All-Glorious,
the All-Forgiving,
   the All-Merciful.

TO STRIVE FOR

From dust to Light
  you shall ascend,
from nothingness to
  eternal Glory
is your destiny, if –
  if you can release the dust.
Release the dust,
  detach yourself
from the pleasures
  and the vanities
and illusions
  of the mortal world;
it does not last,
  that life is fleeting.
Reach for the Light,
  strive to overcome –
for that
  is the measure of success.

ASSIST ME

Oh, Bahá'u'lláh!
Oh, Bahá'u'lláh!
Thou hast awakened me
   and made me conscious
    of Thy Truth and Love
    and Beauty, the Most Great.
How can I serve Thee?
How can I proclaim Thy Cause?
How can I live my life
   to shine Thy Glory?

Oh, Bahá'u'lláh!
Help me,
   for I am weak and frail,
I have no...

Nothing to offer Thee
   but my broken heart
   and wounded soul
   for Thy sake...

SLEEPLESS ONES

The lovers, sleepless
sing of praise, their joy,
of their Beloved
through the night
until dawn
while the world sleeps
heedless
of the blooming rose
in splendor, glory and beauty
in the hearts of men
who rise, sleepless,
to sing
and praise their Lord:
Nightingales of Spirit,
one and all,
circle the Earth
with praise
forever more.

FRAGMENTS

Fragments of their broken lives
and hearts
are offered up
for that is all they have to give.
It is all –
and enough.
Without sacrifice,
there is no gain.
Eternal glory
to outshine the rest
will be theirs
for ever and ever and ever
without end.
What reward
is greater than this?
One wretched life
in exchange –
such bliss!!

FLOWING GRACE

He raineth down a flood of grace
   like pearls and mighty water.
clouds of limitless grace
   have shadowed over you.

The soft-flowing grace of God
   is all around, surrounding you,
a stream of all-embracing grace
   is swirling, twirling about you.

The flood of grace is pouring out
   to all mankind and more,
flowing grace can never cease
   around, beside and in you.

But you must be aware,
   ready and receptive
for this grace to come
   and lift your soul.

You have but to drink your fill
   when you know the thirst.
This hidden and manifest grace
   passes by the blind, unknown.

>

We must seek this grace all times
    from the Lord of Grace Abounding,
so we do not languish
    ignorant of thirst.

Without this grace
    we die like rocks
only fit
    for saints to tread.

SCENTED SHRINE

Roses:
the scent of roses,
roses in vases,
rose petals on the threshold,
roses in the carpet weave:
it is a room of roses.
Roses in the tapestries
hanging on the walls,
roses as decorations,
ornamentation,
rose window panes
over interior doors
and rose
entrance door carvings.
Reminders of Beauty
and traces
of the Traceless Friend:
Roses of God.

WORLDS CONVERGE

A sacred place
where worlds converge
the veil is thin
and, sometimes,
one glimpses through
a moment
transcendent
unreal.
Not truly not-real,
but beyond
the daily "real,"
this physical world.
Contact
with that Reality,
greater than any here,
and thus:
transformation –
however slight.

SHRINE OF THE GATE

That moment in the Tomb
the quiet Tomb
with silent prayers
heartfelt devotion
sobbing breasts
overwhelmed by love,
Divine Love poured
from the Threshold
of His Presence
like a river
unloosed
over me,
my fragile self
unaware,
unprepared,
unknowing.
Divine Love
more than human
can give or wish for:
incomparable Love
as never before experienced;
Love that rocked my being,
in the tomb
not empty
but filled with Spirit
Love
Divine.

HOLY SHRINE

Quiet and peace,
waiting,
for all who enter.
Peace.
Lights.
Lights upon lights
for One condemned
to darkness.
Not even one candle,
and the cold,
so cold
in that prison.
As too, the prison of self,
in darkness,
cold,
ignorance,
and death:
remote from God.

SO FAR AWAY

Sun washed days,
cool night breezes,
   framed and shaped my hours,
   at the Center of the World.

Hours spent in communion,
      contemplation,
      meditation –
   at the Center Holy Spot.

Hours walking dusty streets,
   where holy feet have trod
   at the Center of the World.

Hours spent in longing –
      to know, comprehend, remain
   at the Center of the Heart.

It… is not enough.

My heart yearns, and soul cries out –
      to BE.

To be one –
   with Love,
   with Truth,
   and Beauty.

>

Yet… I cannot.

Words fail…
My pen stops…
I can utter no more…
  In agony…
    So far away.

WHITHER

Whither goest thou
humankind?

Unleash the Gates of Hell
with hate and fear and anger?
Or,
Realize the Promise
of love and hope and peace?

This is the choice –
What do we do?

In our daily lives –
What do we do?

Gales of bombs
destroying cities
and children's lives?
Or,
consultation/cooperation
to rebuild the world?

Our daily actions choose.

SEA OF DEEDS

On the Sea of Deeds
  our lives sail slowly,
one difficulty at a time
  as we define
who we are
  by what we do.

"Let deeds, not words
  be thine adorning,"
for our deeds
  transform our souls.

They are the fruit
  of our lives
and evidence
  of faith.

Deeds transform us
  from who we are,
to the soul
  we can become.

FULFILLMENT

We see the intention of the years,
    man's plans dismayed
  God's plan fulfilled
    through centuries and cycles.
Today is the growing
    of the seed long planted.
  The fruit is yet to come,
    centuries in future.
We have a part,
    each and every one,
  our choice,
    our destiny.
Some do not fulfill,
    others rise to Glory,
  as we try and strive
    to carry on.

Please God,
  we may achieve!

HERESY PROGRESS

The heresy vision
adopted and sustained
by faithful few
despite
ridicule, suffering, persecution
endured.
More followed,
enamored,
carried on The Vision
and worked
to make it real.
Generations later,
populations base their lives
on The Vision
and couldn't imagine
life without –
resulting
in human progress.

WORLD OF ONENESS

The world of One Mind,
    One Heart,
    One Soul,
    One Love,
 One Love of the One Creator.

Unity of Voice,
    expression:
"Praise and Glory to God,
    The All-Glorious."

Ages and cycles
    turn and sway,
today is the birth of God's new Way.

One planet united in One Love,
  all colors, nations and truths.

Beginning of The Peace,
    at last…
Praise be to Thee,
    Oh, God.

TIMES, NOW

Time doesn't answer,
  it passes by
    slowly or lurching
  we never know.
People, bewildered,
  longing for assurance:
    life was good once,
  but they forget,
Forget the uncertainties
  that were survived
    by others
  not affecting them,
And uncertainties now
  will pass in time
    forgotten;
  only our progress
Will be noted and envied:
  that so much could be done
    by so few
  and so tried.
It is not who we are
  but what we do
    despite
  the uncertainties now.
Change is painful
  but necessary
    for the *now* to be bettered
  for future,

>

Because our striving
  is our salvation
    and the world's,
  and victory
Will come
  on the wings
    of exhaustion
  and hope.

TRANSFORMATION

The Point of Utter Helplessness
   is a bewilderment
   or nonsense,
   to those of yet
   not reached it.
To the one who has arrived,
   that Point
   is a line divide:
   life before –
   nothing after.
That Point erases
   ones self;
   all
   that you thought you were –
   is gone.
The Void of Helplessness
   swallows you,
   consumes
   all that you knew
   you were.
Questions come:
   What to do?
   Where to turn?
   What to learn?
   Who am I now?

>

Eventually,
   a part of life
   can be rebuilt
   over wreckage
   and debris.
It is a different life
   because you are
   a different soul,
   who has been tested
   and transformed:
Now a new creation.

THE KING OF GLORY REIGNS

Mounted on His Throne
of imperishable Glory
and Dominion,
the King of Glory Reigns
over hearts and minds
of millions
formerly contentious,
hating, killing,
now lovers raising children
of a new creation
slowly transforming the world
into a new Eden
where all
are embraced with Love.
The King of Glory Reigns
and we rejoice
for the Age of Peace
has come.

SOUL JOURNEY

The journey of the soul
   unwinds, rewinds,
expands, compresses
   and continues to change.
The growing soul alters
   perception and direction
seeking the open way
   despite difficulties and trials.
The adventurer knows
   behind whirlwind lies calm,
past chaos is peace,
   beyond torment is grace.
The traveler sees above
   apparent limits,
the valleys of illusions
   to the mountains of certitude.
Within the heart, tenderly,
   the seekers carries hope
and listens to the quiet whispers:
   "peace."
Temptations abound
   to give up, relax and forget,
but Truth
   is a higher goal.
Distractions continually assail
   the earnest one,
but stamina is exercised
   and prevails.

>

Eventually...
   the height of attainment
is achieved
   and the vista is clear.
Up ahead, through the mist,
   another goal is perceived,
for growth
   never ends...

CHOICES

Formed from dust
nourished by Light
torn
between two realms –
matter and Spirit,
thus
we live our lives.

Tension forms our choices:
self, or other?
dust, or Light?
Our choice:
reach for the Light?
or, hold to dust?
be helpful?
or, serve self?

Actions define our lives –
and form our souls.

Our choice: self, or other?

STRUGGLE TO THE DISTANT SHORE

The passions of life surge 'round us
  pulling one way,
  urging another,
  pleading…
Yet, we can not follow
  for the depths are great
  and we are not strong.
To swim against the current
  is tiring,
  but it is the only way
  to reach the shore.
Millions pass by (and die)
  on their way of ease
  and ignorance,
But we aim higher,
  above the norm,
  for there is firm footing
    and reunion.

It is Reunion that pulls us on:
  Reunion
    with joy and love and exaltation,
  Reunion
    with all that is most wonderful,
  Reunion
    beyond all I know now,

>

Reunion
    that will embrace and lift the soul,
Reunion
    that will banish all pain,
Reunion
    when I can finally rest.

In that hope
  I carry on,
Struggle
  and strive to attain,

The Distant Shore.

THE APPEARANCE

The pilgrim,
forgetful of promise:
'attain the Threshold
is the same
as entering My Presence.'
Pilgrim simply
seeks to give
his heart and mind and soul
to his Beloved.
An act
of renunciation,
selfless supreme.
Amidst tears
a Light shines
Power Restrained
from the empty tomb,
the Room of Glory.
Pilgrim knows love
more powerful than Earth.
Tears abound:
"Why me, Lord?
Why me?"

Brief moment
forever stilled
into his heart,
his soul
forever more.

GL-LXXXII

A soul,
after its ascension
from this physical life,
which had remained
faithful and steadfast
through tests and trials,
shall,
at the bidding
of Almighty God,
provide and supply
power, inspiration, energy,
to those here,
through whom
arts and wonders of the world
are made manifest
and
attain realization
in this physical world.

SACRIFICIAL LIFE

A living martyr
aching
day by day,
hour by hour,
moment by moment
for that which cannot
fully be attained:
detachment,
the goal,
from transitory world –
for love of God
which promises:
joy,
exaltation
and glory
for ever
and ever
without end.

TRACES TO REMAIN

Traces,
some have left traces
of their dedication
and devotion.
Some we know,
a few, a tiny few;
God knows more –
legions are vast.
How can we too,
in their footsteps,
follow?
And in time,
leave traces
of our own?

With resolve and volition,
dedication and devotion,
we can take those steps
if we but try.

BEYOND THE BARRIER

Live a life.
Create a life –
  or lives.
Save a life –
  or lives.
Write
  to enrich
  lives far,
  far from your own.
Breathe,
  slowly –
  calm
  the mind.
We shall see
  in the end,
  after the end,
Accomplishments
  despite trials
  and afflictions.
We are blind
  here
  to reality,
  oneness,
  and love.
Once we know:
  explosions
  of JOY!!

ASPIRATION TO ATTAIN

Voices that are seeking,
voices that are reaching,
  beyond time,
  beyond pain,
    to oneness,
    to growth,
    to authentic self.

Transcending the pain,
transcending the wounds,
transcending confusion
  of a world that has lost
    its balance
    and order
    and beauty
    and truth.

Poets cry
  and souls respond, react
  and return the cry:
    we are here,
    we are not alone,
    we are real,
    we are real,
    we are true.

>

This age of pain,
this loneliness,
  will not persist,
  will not endure,
  can not sustain
    itself
    or any other.

It is the change that is real,
  the struggle,
  the effort
    from self
    toward
true poverty
  and absolute
    nothingness.

The goal of extinction
  in the sea
  in the love
  in the name
    Bahá'u'lláh
    the Most Great.

I die content.

LIFE OF BAHÁ'U'LLÁH

LIFE OF BAHÁ'U'LLÁH

Bahá'u'lláh, a title meaning 'the Glory of God,'
like the title 'Christ' given to Yeshua (also
spelled Eashoa), more commonly known as
Jesus, was named Husayn Ali. He was born on
12 November 1817 in Tehran, the capital of
Persia, now Iran, the son of a wealthy govern-
ment minister. The family could trace its
lineage back to great Persian kings centuries
before.

He was born into a life of wealth and ease. As
typical of the upper class, His education con-
sisted of calligraphy, classical Persian poetry,
horsemanship and swordsmanship. Others could
be paid for their knowledge of other subjects, if
they were ever needed. His formal education
was quite limited, yet as a teenager He gained a
reputation for His knowledge. He could solve
problems brought to him and His judgment
gained a wide reputation. Even religious scho-
lars would come to hear His explanations of
religious subjects.

He did not give His attention to acquiring more
wealth or showing off His skills with the horse
or sword, but concerned Himself with conditions

of the poor. As a young boy He was willing to give away the family sheep to those who had none. By the time He was in His thirties, He was known as 'father of the poor.' When His father's position came open at the royal court and was offered to Him, He declined to accept. In 1844 a young merchant attracted attention by claiming that long-awaited promises of God were about to be fulfilled. He called Himself, the Báb (bob), meaning 'the Gate.' These claims spread across the country, finding ready ears among all classes. As soon as Bahá'u'lláh read some of His writings, He instantly recognized in them the same Divine Power and authority as in the Qur'án and became a follower.

Four years later, Bahá'u'lláh was arrested for being a follower of the Báb and tortured with the bastinado. The soles of His bare feet were beaten with a rod. This was one of the lighter punishments of the day. He had attempted to join some other Bábís who were being attacked by the army.

In 1850 the Báb was executed and most of His leading followers hunted down and also killed. The government was trying to erase the movement. Because of His social status, Bahá'u'lláh was spared, but He was falsely charged with complicity to assassinate the Shah. He did not run from the soldiers sent to arrest Him, but went to meet them to demonstrate His inno-

cence. He was forced to walk, on foot, to The-
ran in the hot sun. News of His arrest traveled
ahead of Him and people came to see His humil-
iation. Many along the way threw stones and
other objects at Him, often garbage or other foul
matter.

In Tehran He was thrown into a dungeon, built
to be a cistern for water, known as the Black Pit.
It was well known for its foul conditions – no
light, no fresh air, no plumbing. Prisoners were
closely chained together in two rows along its
sides. They had to sit in their own wastes. In
this place, Bahá'u'lláh received the first visions
of His Revelation. He later described it brought
to Him by the Maid of Heaven, the Holy Spirit.
He said the Revelation poured over Him like a
river.

After four months in this prison it was proved
that He was innocent. For His innocence He
was exiled from the country for the rest of His
life. All of His lands and properties were taken
from Him and the family was instantly impover-
ished. Without being able to recuperate from the
treatment in the prison, the weight of the chains
around His neck caused severe wounds, He and
his family were forced to leave Persia.

They were sent to Baghdad in the Ottoman Em-
pire. The winter journey, much of it through
snow-covered mountains, took three months.

Pack animals were their only transportation, as well as walking themselves. They were ill-clothed, poorly sheltered and without sufficient food. Their sufferings during the trip were unforgettable.

Finally, in April 1853, they arrived in Baghdad. When other Bábís learned of His location, they began to turn to Bahá'u'lláh with their questions and concerns. They found in His Writings the same spirit as in the Writings of the Báb. This caused jealousy in His half-brother who became contentious. After a year, Bahá'u'lláh left the city alone and lived solitary, as a dervish in the mountains of Kurdistan. There, He came to grips with the Revelation He had begun to receive, His future public role and the consequences. He remained for two years until the reputation of a remarkable dervish reached Baghdad and His family knew it must be Him.

During these two years spent in meditation and reflection, Bahá'u'lláh pondered the Revelation He had received in prison and what it might mean for Himself, His family and the world. It was a time of preparation. So far, He had told no one about the Revelation.

A representative from the family was sent to search for this dervish and implore Him to return to Baghdad. This He did in 1856. He set about encouraging and reviving the followers of the

Báb. The condition and stature of the Bábís increased and His reputation as a spiritual leader spread even wider. Some of Bahá'u'lláh's most significant works were written in this time, such as the *Book of Certitude* explaining the interconnection of Jewish, Christian and Muslim scriptures, as well as the *Hidden Words*, condensed statements of eternal spiritual truths.

In April 1863 the Sultan of the Ottoman Empire, at the urging of the Persian government, exiled Bahá'u'lláh further from the border to Constantinople (now Istanbul). On the eve of this departure so many came to bid farewell that He moved temporarily to a garden. In the decade spent in the city His fame had increased to such an extent that news of this further banishment generated an upwelling of public loss. Government officials, academics, clerics and common people were united in their grief.

This time in the garden is regarded by Bahá'ís as the Most Holy Festival. The garden was named Riḍván, or Paradise, because of this time. While there, Bahá'u'lláh informed His closest followers of His Revelation. The time is commemorated for twelve days, the length of time He spent in the garden, every year by Bahá'ís. It is known as the Festival of Riḍván.

Bahá'u'lláh was in Constantinople only a few months before He and His family were forced to relocate again. This time, to Adrianople (Edirne), where they arrived before the end of 1863. This journey took just less than two weeks, but those weeks occurred during the coldest winter in nearly half a century. Needless to say, its rigors blurred into that earlier winter journey so many years before.

Again, in Adrianople, once the people got to know Bahá'u'lláh, His character, dignity, and wisdom attracted them to Him. He was sought by government officials, including the Governor himself, scholars and clerics and ordinary people for His advice and insight. He was shown such reverence that even walking through the streets people would stop and bow in respect to Him. Their adoration was obvious.

All was not well, though. The jealously of his half-brother never abated, in fact, it intensified. Finally, the brother hired an assassin to poison Bahá'u'lláh. The amount should have killed Him, but only made Him extremely ill which took months to recover. Nerve damage was permanent, though. For the rest of His life there was a tremor in His hand which affected His handwriting. An unexpected benefit of this was that His Writings are easily identifiable from this date forward.

While in Adrianople, beginning in 1867, and finishing the next year in Akka, Bahá'u'lláh wrote letters to the most powerful kings and rulers. These included: Napoleon III, Queen Victoria, Kaiser Wilhelm I, Tsar Alexander II, Emperor Franz Joseph, Pope Pius IX, Ottoman Sultan Abdul-Aziz, and Nasiri'd-Din Shah of Persia. In these letters He openly proclaims His station as a Messenger of God, urges them to uphold justice in their realms, and encourages them to form a commonwealth of nations where mutual disarmament would be possible. He warns of catastrophe if they don't. They did not and the history we know was the result.

In 1868 Bahá'u'lláh was further banished to Akka, at the extreme isolated edge of the Otto-man Empire. This prison city was so remote from any important centers that it was assumed His influence would die out – if the prisoners survived. Generally, sentence to this penal colony was a sentence of death itself. The city was unhealthy, had no fresh water and the air was so foul it was said birds would die in flight overhead. Representatives of foreign govern-ments were so concerned that several offered to intervene on His behalf. He declined their assistance, not wanting to cause an international incident.

For this banishment the prisoners would be split. The actions of the half-brother were so fractious he and his family would be sent to Cyprus. The rest were sent to Akka. Some followers of each, though, were assigned to the other camp. The oriental mind considered this a just punishment.

The last stretch of this journey was by boat across the Mediterranean and the Bay of Haifa. The last segment was done in a very cramped sailboat which became becalmed in the middle of the bay on a hot summer's day. They spent eight hours with inadequate food and water under the burning sun. When they finally reached the city, the prisoners were pelted with garbage and verbal abuse from the population. This attitude was only reinforced when the official decree of perpetual banishment from the Sultan was read to the public. There was to be no interaction between the prisoners and the population, ever!

Yet, again, the same transformation occurred in the local population as had happened in every other city. Gradually officials began to treat Bahá'u'lláh with respect and the rest of the population followed.

Two years after their arrival, Bahá'u'lláh's youngest son fell through a skylight of the prison. He had been on the roof walking and praying. The skylight was simply an opening in the roof and he missed his step. He fell onto crates below and died of his injuries. He asked his father if his life could be accepted as a means for their restrictions to be relaxed. Shortly after that, the family was allowed to move to a house in the city and pilgrims were allowed into the city to see Bahá'u'lláh.

Locals, as well as pilgrims, came to ask advice. The Governor of the city asked if he could assist Bahá'u'lláh in some way. He replied that the aqueduct, which had formerly brought fresh water into the city, could be repaired. This was speedily accomplished. Local residents remarked that even the climate of the city had improved.

Local officials began to speak of Bahá'u'lláh leaving the city, in contradiction to the decree of banishment. In 1877, curious if this might be possible, Bahá'u'lláh's oldest son, 'Abdu'l-Bahá, secured permission from the owner of a grove of trees outside of town for His use. He planned a banquet there to which local notables were invited. Their acceptance indicated the decree was a dead letter.

A house outside the city was then rented for Bahá'u'lláh and later that year He left the confines of the city after nine years there of imprisonment or house arrest. Two years later, a larger house nearby was rented and Bahá'u'lláh lived there the last few years of His life. He was buried in a building on the grounds which is now regarded by Bahá'ís as the Most Holy Spot.

In His Writings, Bahá'u'lláh not only gave guidance for an individual's life, but also for community administration, and steps to global peace. He outlined how His followers should organize their collective affairs. He also appointed His oldest son, 'Abdu'l-Bahá, to be His successor, the central authority to turn to. These features, known as the Covenant of Bahá'u'lláh, as well as the fact of the Scriptures being in His own handwriting, are unique in religious history. The result is a unified global community of believers working together to improve their lives, their families, their local communities and the world.

Notes:

BÁB, BÁBÍ – Prophet-Herald of the Bahá'í
Faith (1819-1850), meaning 'the Gate' (to God),
and designation of His followers. He was ex-
ecuted for His heretical teachings, such as the
equality of men and women.

BEST BELOVED OF THE WORLDS –
Bahá'u'lláh wrote to the Shah of Persia of His
experience while receiving revelation. He
quoted this in His letter to Shaykh Muhammad
Taqí-i-Najafi whose father had owed money to
two brothers, prominent citizens of his town.
Instead of paying off the debt, he denounced the
two as being Bábís, betrayers of Islam, causing
mobs to strip them of their considerable posses-
sions, even to the plants in their gardens. Their
death sentence was obtained, proceeded by
torture. The two are now known to history as
the King of Martyrs and the Beloved of Martyrs.
Because of these actions of the father the letter
to the son is titled: *Epistle to the Son of the Wolf.*

A GLIMPSE IN TIME – The "quote" in this
poem, at the time the poem was written, was
considered part of Bahá'í scripture. Efforts at
the Bahá'í World Center to authentic the source
have determined that it is not.

GLORY – reference to Bahá'u'lláh.

113

MAID OF HEAVEN – personification of the
Holy Spirit in Bahá'í Sacred Scriptures.

NIGHTENGALE OF PARADISE – reference to
Bahá'u'lláh.

QUOTES – are from Bahá'í Sacred Texts except
for those in the poems: Golden Alchemy, Sur-
render, Here Am I, and individual words.

RIḌVÁN – Arabic for "Paradise. Twelve day
festival commemorating Bahá'u'lláh's declara-
tion of His mission to His companions in 1863
in the Garden of Riḍván in Baghdad.

ROSE, ROSE OF GLORY – reference to
Bahá'u'lláh.

SUPPLICATION – a prayer revealed by the Báb
set in verse form.

YEAR HIN – Hin is a designation for the
number 68 in the Abjad system of assigning a
number value to letters of the alphabet. It was a
kind of code. The number 68 referred to the
year 1268 according to the Muslim calendar
which corresponds with 1851-52. This reference
was confirmed and repeated by the Báb. It was
that year when Bahá'u'lláh received the first
indications of His mission. In some places it is
also referred to as the "year nine," being nine
years after the Declaration of the Báb.

Credits:

Prairies of Possibilities: Lightly Treading, In the Darkness Shines, Genesis II, Soul Monarch, In Wonder, Quiet and Peace, Surrender, Times Now, Transformation, Golden Alchemy, Soul Journey, Struggle to the Distant Shore, Supplication, Angels in Separation, Sea of Deeds

Sweet Scented Streams: Bahá'u'lláh, Best Beloved of the Worlds, Please God!, Soaring Bird, For the Glory of Thy Name, Door of Grace, To Strive, With Me, Invocation, Desert Growing, Fulfillment, World of Oneness.

Voices From a Borrowed Garden: Aspiration to Attain, Steadfastness

Whispers Shouting Glory: A Glimpse in Time, Garden of the Rose, Silent Footsteps Passing, Soul Soaring, So Far Away

World Order: Sun Magnificent.

Index of Titles

Index of First Lines

.

www.ingramcontent.com/pod-product-compliance
Lightning Source LLC
Chambersburg PA
CBHW031516040426
42445CB00009B/258